World Atlas

Grades K-3

 Macmillan/McGraw-Hill

Contents

The World: Continents and Oceans

ARCTIC OCEAN

NORTH
AMERICA

ATLANTIC
OCEAN

PACIFIC
OCEAN

SOUTH
AMERICA

ATLANTIC
OCEAN

ANTARCTICA

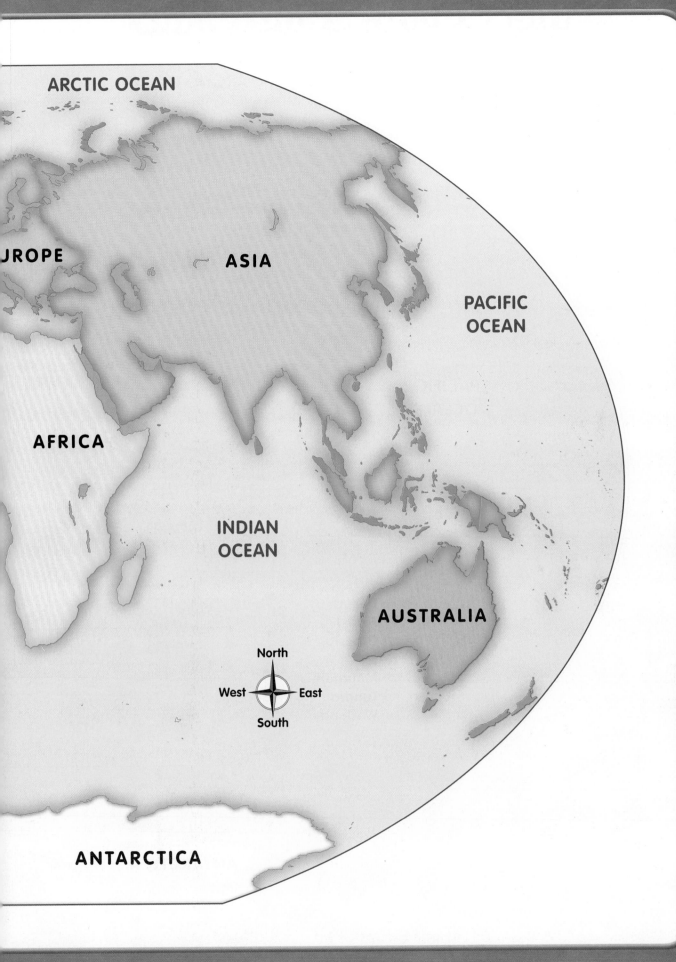

ARCTIC OCEAN

EUROPE

ASIA

PACIFIC
OCEAN

AFRICA

INDIAN
OCEAN

AUSTRALIA

North
West — East
South

ANTARCTICA

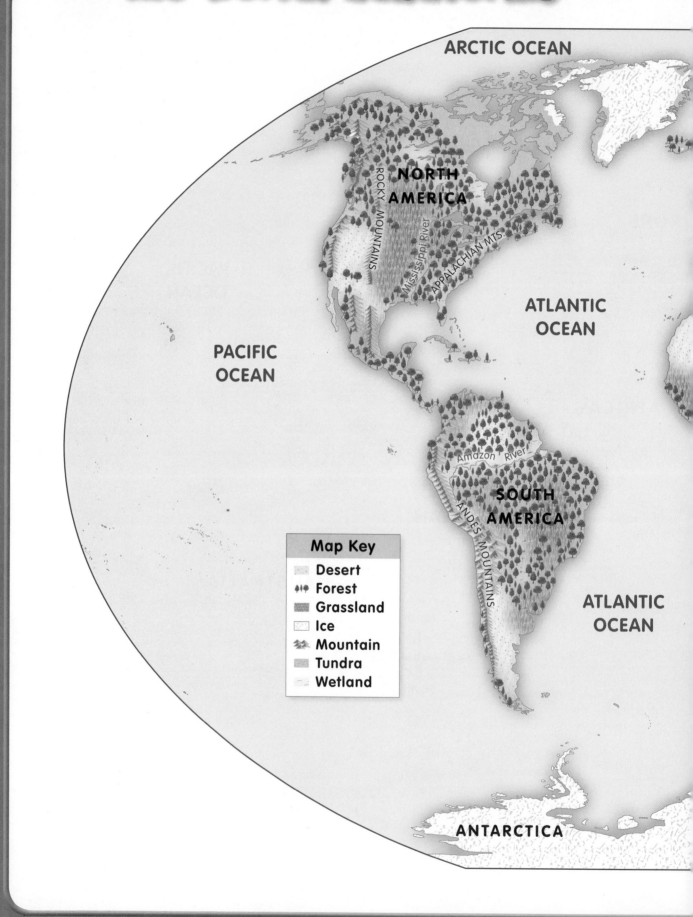

ARCTIC OCEAN

NORTH
AMERICA

ROCKY MOUNTAINS

Mississippi River

APPALACHIAN MTS.

ATLANTIC
OCEAN

PACIFIC
OCEAN

Amazon River

SOUTH
AMERICA

ANDES MOUNTAINS

ATLANTIC
OCEAN

Map Key

	Desert
	Forest
	Grassland
	Ice
	Mountain
	Tundra
	Wetland

ANTARCTICA

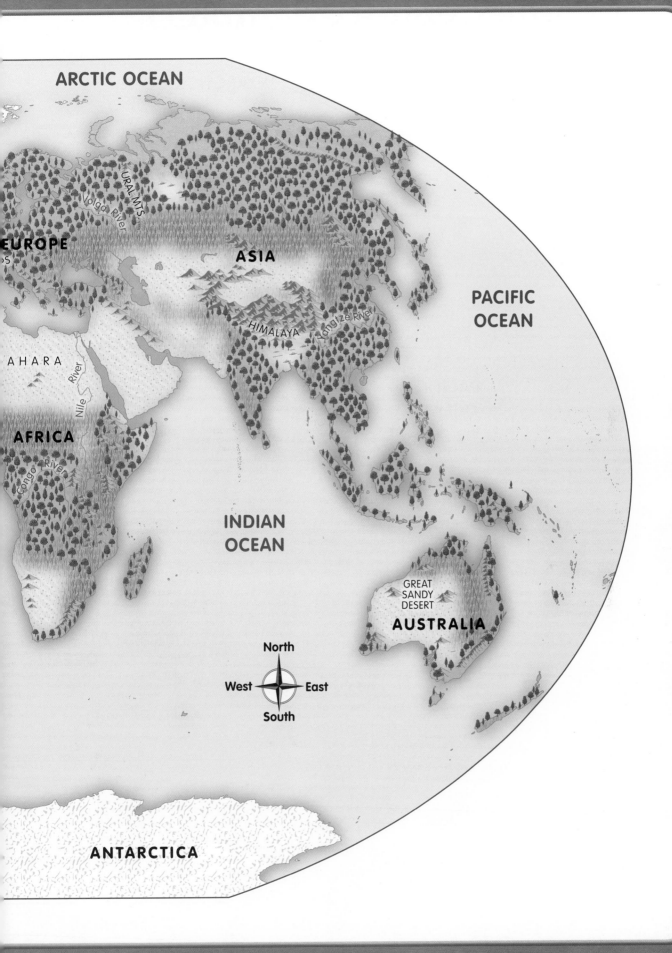

ARCTIC OCEAN

EUROPE

URAL MTS

Volga River

ASIA

PACIFIC
OCEAN

AHARA

River

Nile

HIMALAYA

Yangtze River

AFRICA

Congo River

INDIAN
OCEAN

GREAT
SANDY
DESERT

AUSTRALIA

North

West ✦ East

South

ANTARCTICA

The World: Countries

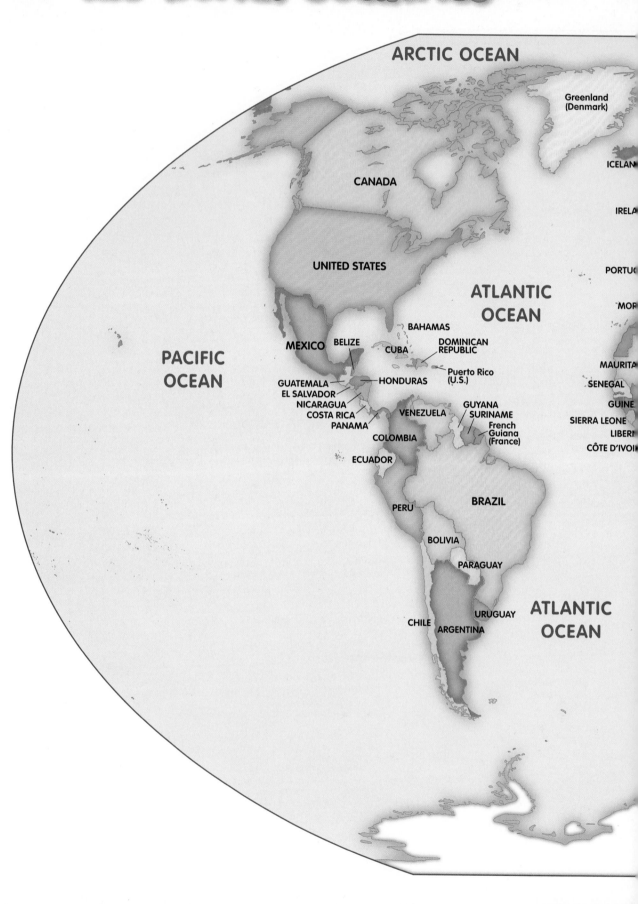

ARCTIC OCEAN

Greenland (Denmark)

ICELAN

CANADA

IRELA

UNITED STATES

PORTU

ATLANTIC OCEAN

MOR

BAHAMAS

PACIFIC OCEAN

MEXICO BELIZE

DOMINICAN REPUBLIC

CUBA

MAURITA

Puerto Rico (U.S.)

SENEGAL

GUATEMALA HONDURAS

GUINE

EL SALVADOR

NICARAGUA

GUYANA

SIERRA LEONE

COSTA RICA

SURINAME

LIBER

PANAMA

VENEZUELA

French Guiana (France)

CÔTE D'IVOI

COLOMBIA

ECUADOR

PERU

BRAZIL

BOLIVIA

PARAGUAY

ATLANTIC OCEAN

URUGUAY

CHILE ARGENTINA

ARCTIC OCEAN

NORWAY

SWEDEN
FINLAND

RUSSIA

BELARUS
POLAND
GERMANY   UKRAINE

KAZAKHSTAN

MONGOLIA

ROMANIA

UZBEKISTAN   KYRGYZSTAN

NORTH
KOREA

ITALY

TURKEY   TURKMENISTAN   TAJIKISTAN

JAPAN

SOUTH
KOREA

GREECE

SYRIA

CHINA

PACIFIC
OCEAN

TUNISIA

ISRAEL   IRAQ   IRAN

AFGHANISTAN

LIBYA   EGYPT   SAUDI
ARABIA

PAKISTAN   NEPAL

BANGLADESH   MYANMAR
(BURMA)

TAIWAN

OMAN   INDIA

NIGER   CHAD   SUDAN   YEMEN

THAILAND   VIETNAM   PHILIPPINES

NIGERIA   CENTRAL
AFRICAN
REPUBLIC

ETHIOPIA   SOMALIA

SRI
LANKA

CAMEROON

KENYA

MALAYSIA

GABON   DEMOCRATIC
REPUBLIC
OF THE
CONGO   TANZANIA

CONGO

INDONESIA   PAPUA
NEW
GUINEA

SOLOMON
ISLANDS

ANGOLA   ZAMBIA

INDIAN
OCEAN

ZIMBABWE

MADAGASCAR

VANUATU   FIJI
ISLANDS

BOTSWANA

NAMIBIA

MOZAMBIQUE

AUSTRALIA

SOUTH
AFRICA

North

West ✦ East

South

NEW
ZEALAND

ANTARCTICA

The United States: Landforms

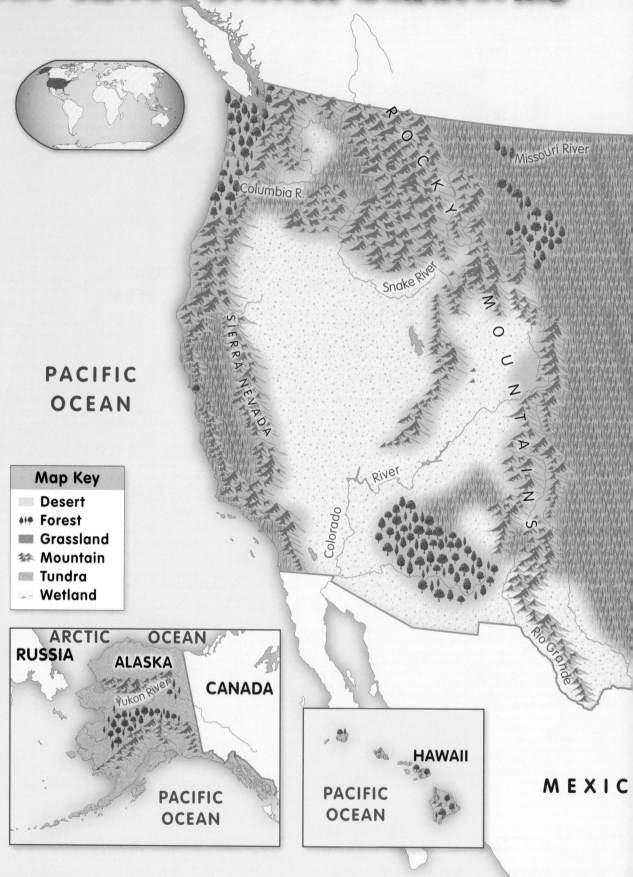

PACIFIC
OCEAN

Map Key
- Desert
- Forest
- Grassland
- Mountain
- Tundra
- Wetland

ROCKY

MOUNTAINS

SIERRA NEVADA

Missouri River

Columbia R.

Snake River

River

Colorado

Rio Grande

ARCTIC OCEAN

RUSSIA

ALASKA

CANADA

Yukon River

PACIFIC
OCEAN

HAWAII

PACIFIC
OCEAN

MEXIC

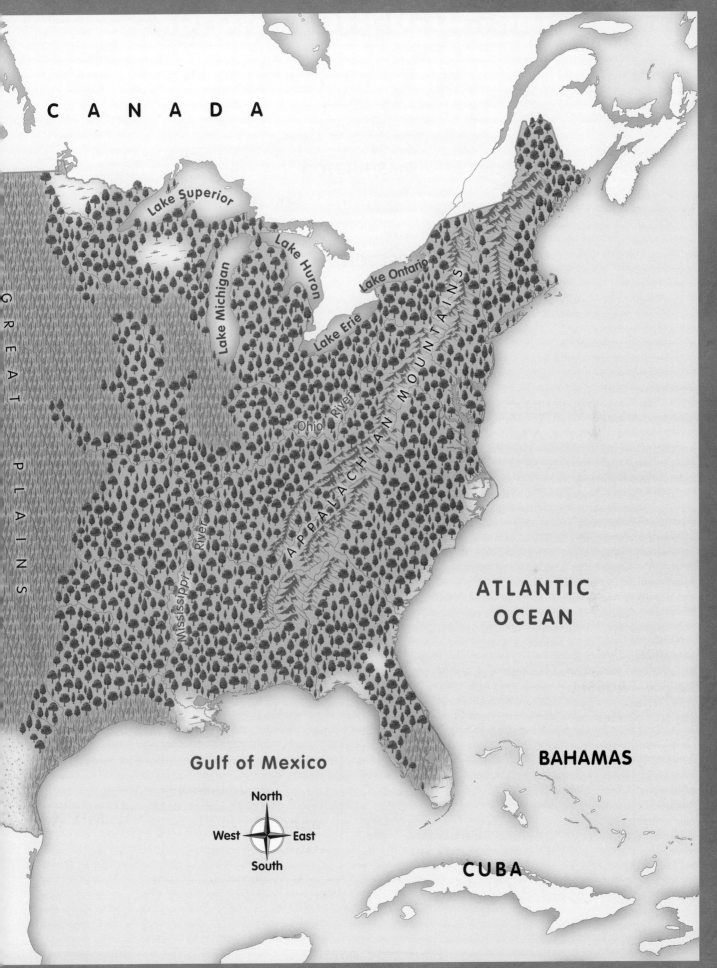

CANADA

GREAT PLAINS

Lake Superior

Lake Michigan

Lake Huron

Lake Ontario

Lake Erie

APPALACHIAN MOUNTAINS

Ohio River

Mississippi River

ATLANTIC OCEAN

Gulf of Mexico

BAHAMAS

CUBA

North

West — East

South

The 50 United States

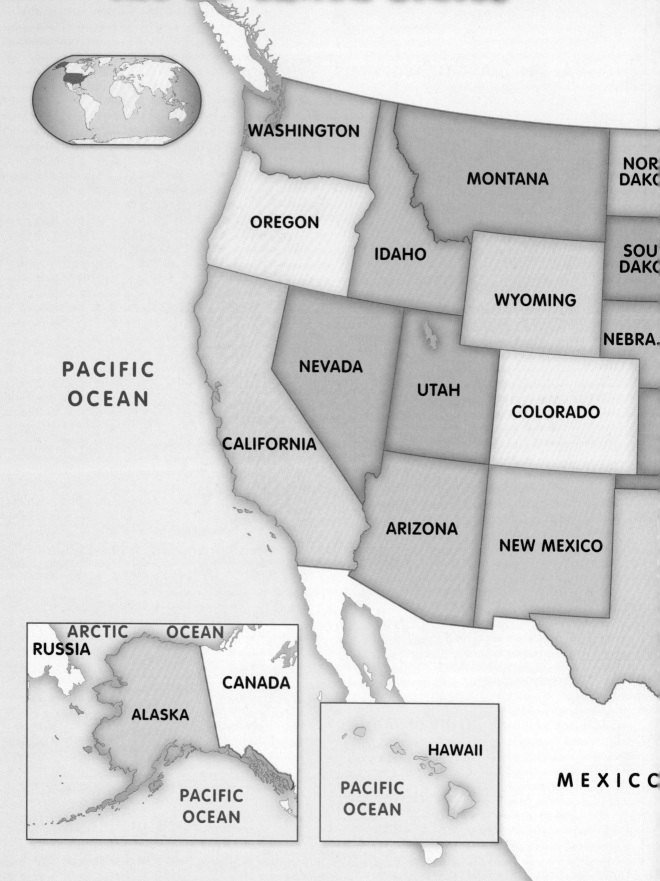

WASHINGTON

MONTANA

NOR...
DAKO...

OREGON

IDAHO

SOU...
DAKO...

WYOMING

NEBRA...

PACIFIC
OCEAN

NEVADA

UTAH

COLORADO

CALIFORNIA

ARIZONA

NEW MEXICO

ARCTIC OCEAN

RUSSIA

CANADA

ALASKA

PACIFIC
OCEAN

HAWAII

PACIFIC
OCEAN

MEXICO

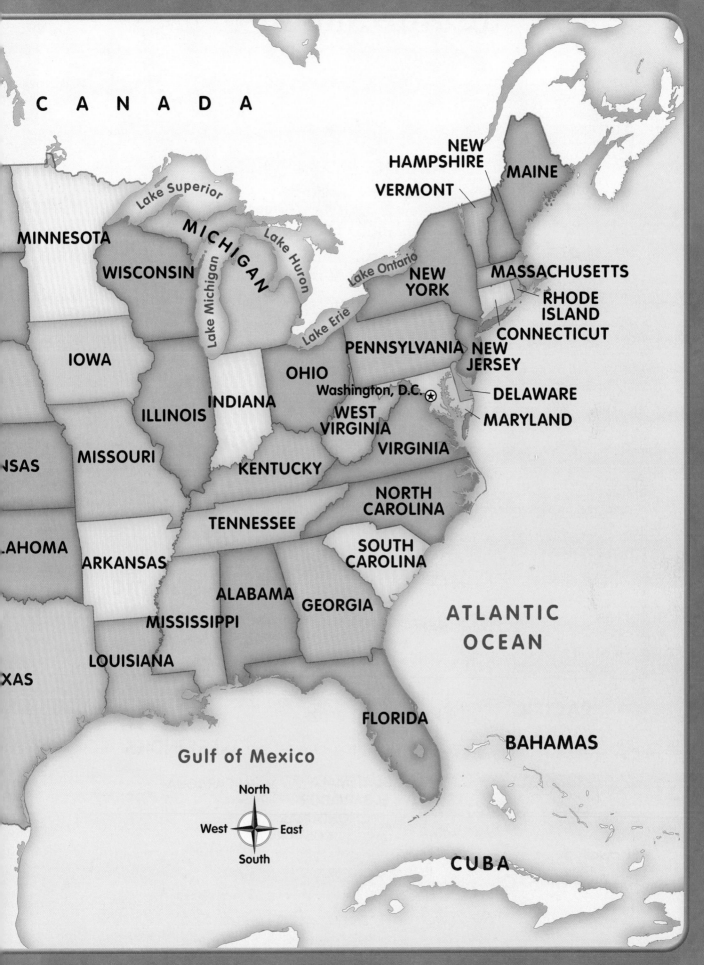

CANADA

MINNESOTA

WISCONSIN

Lake Superior

MICHIGAN

Lake Michigan

Lake Huron

Lake Ontario

Lake Erie

NEW
HAMPSHIRE

VERMONT

MAINE

MASSACHUSETTS

NEW
YORK

RHODE
ISLAND

CONNECTICUT

IOWA

OHIO

PENNSYLVANIA NEW
JERSEY

Washington, D.C. ⊛

DELAWARE

INDIANA

ILLINOIS

WEST
VIRGINIA

MARYLAND

MISSOURI

KENTUCKY

VIRGINIA

NSAS

NORTH
CAROLINA

AHOMA

TENNESSEE

ARKANSAS

SOUTH
CAROLINA

ALABAMA

GEORGIA

MISSISSIPPI

ATLANTIC
OCEAN

LOUISIANA

XAS

FLORIDA

BAHAMAS

Gulf of Mexico

North

West ✦ East

South

CUBA

13

North America

ARCTIC OCEAN

Greenland (Denmark)

Alaska (U.S.)

CANADA

North
West   East
South

UNITED STATES

ATLANTIC OCEAN

PACIFIC OCEAN

MEXICO   BELIZE

WEST INDIES

GUATEMALA
EL SALVADOR
HONDURAS
COSTA RICA

NICARAGUA

PANAMA

Hawaii (U.S.)

South America

ATLANTIC
OCEAN

VENEZUELA

GUYANA
SURINAME
French Guiana
(France)

COLOMBIA

Galápagos
Islands
(Ecuador)

ECUADOR

PERU

BRAZIL

BOLIVIA

PACIFIC
OCEAN

PARAGUAY

CHILE

ARGENTINA

URUGUAY

North

West — East

South

ATLANTIC
OCEAN

Falkland Islands
(U.K.)

South
Georgia
(U.K.)

Europe

ARCTIC OCEAN

ICELAND

North
West — East
South

NORWAY

North
Sea

IRELAND   UNITED
KINGDOM   DENMARK

ATLANTIC   NETHERLANDS
OCEAN

BELGIUM   GERMANY

LUXEMBOURG   CZEC
REPUB

FRANCE   LIECHTENSTEIN

SWITZERLAND   AUSTF

SLOVEN

CRO

ANDORRA

MONACO   SAN
PORTUGAL   MARINO

SPAIN   ITAL

Mediterranean Sea

MALTA

Canary Islands
(Spain)

WEDEN

FINLAND

Baltic Sea

ESTONIA

LATVIA

LITHUANIA

BELARUS

OLAND

UKRAINE

OVAKIA

MOLDOVA

UNGARY

ROMANIA

BOSNIA AND
HERZEGOVINA

SERBIA

BULGARIA

MONTENEGRO

MACEDONIA

LBANIA

GREECE

Black Sea

Italian girl
near the Alps

Asia

North
West — East
South

ARCTIC

GEORGIA

TURKEY
ARMENIA — AZERBAIJAN

KAZAKHSTAN

CYPRUS
LEBANON   SYRIA

UZBEKISTAN

TURKMENISTAN   KYRGYZSTA

West Bank

ISRAEL
JORDAN   IRAQ

TAJIKISTA

IRAN   AFGHANISTAN

KUWAIT

SAUDI
ARABIA

BAHRAIN
QATAR

PAKISTAN

UNITED ARAB
EMIRATES   OMAN

IND

YEMEN

Carrying a dragon in a Chinese New
Year Parade

SRI
LANKA

MALDIVES

INDIAN
OCEAN

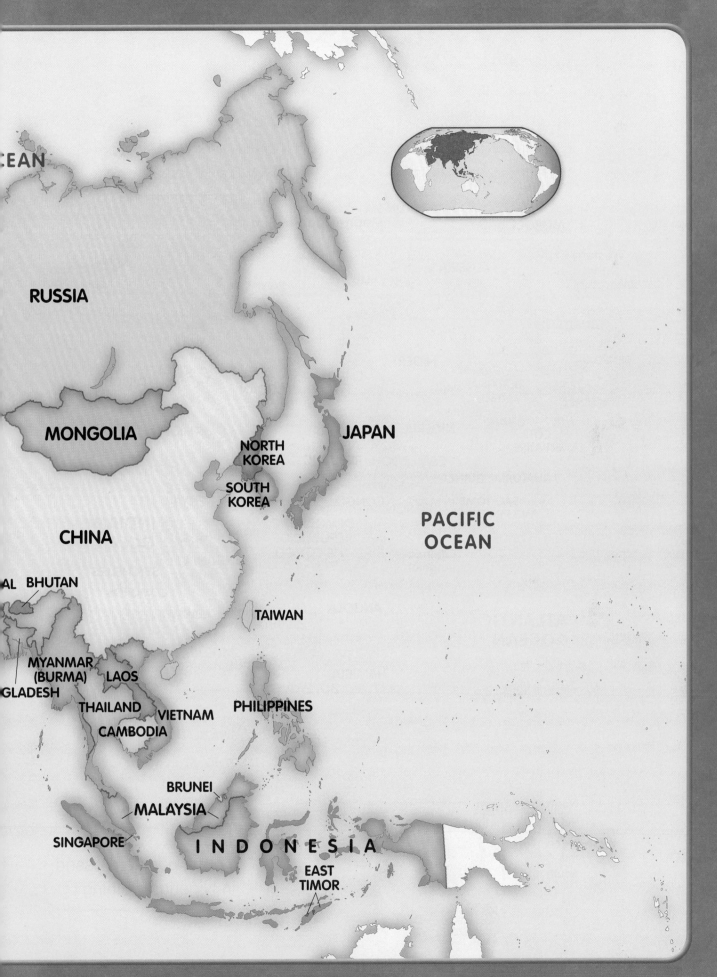

OCEAN

RUSSIA

MONGOLIA

CHINA

NORTH
KOREA

SOUTH
KOREA

JAPAN

PACIFIC
OCEAN

AL BHUTAN

TAIWAN

MYANMAR
(BURMA) LAOS
GLADESH

THAILAND
VIETNAM

CAMBODIA

PHILIPPINES

BRUNEI
MALAYSIA

SINGAPORE

I N D O N E S I A

EAST
TIMOR

Africa

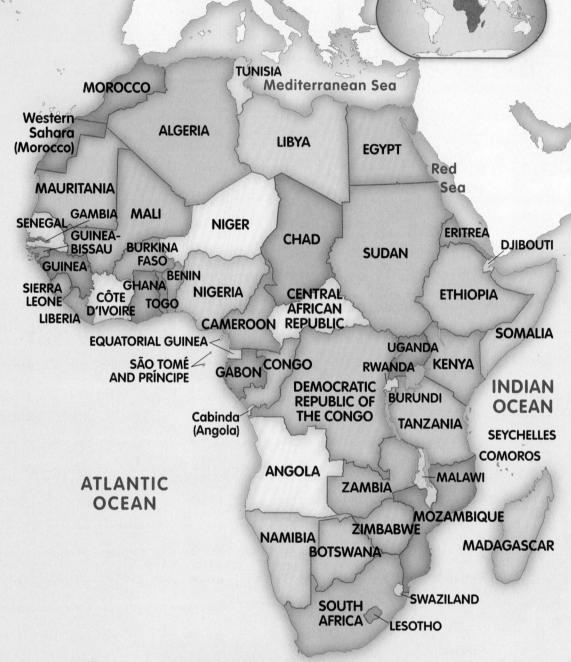

MOROCCO

TUNISIA

Mediterranean Sea

Western Sahara (Morocco)

ALGERIA

LIBYA

EGYPT

Red Sea

MAURITANIA

SENEGAL

GAMBIA

MALI

NIGER

CHAD

SUDAN

ERITREA

DJIBOUTI

GUINEA-BISSAU

BURKINA FASO

GUINEA

BENIN

SIERRA LEONE

GHANA

CÔTE D'IVOIRE

TOGO

NIGERIA

CENTRAL AFRICAN REPUBLIC

ETHIOPIA

LIBERIA

CAMEROON

SOMALIA

EQUATORIAL GUINEA

UGANDA

SÃO TOMÉ AND PRÍNCIPE

GABON

CONGO

RWANDA

KENYA

DEMOCRATIC REPUBLIC OF THE CONGO

BURUNDI

INDIAN OCEAN

Cabinda (Angola)

TANZANIA

SEYCHELLES

COMOROS

ATLANTIC OCEAN

ANGOLA

ZAMBIA

MALAWI

MOZAMBIQUE

ZIMBABWE

MADAGASCAR

NAMIBIA

BOTSWANA

SWAZILAND

SOUTH AFRICA

LESOTHO

North

West — East

South

Young people dressed in Nigerian clothing

Australia and Oceania

PALAU

MARSHALL
ISLANDS

FEDERATED STATES
OF MICRONESIA

KIRIBATI

NAURU

PAPUA
NEW GUINEA

SOLOMON
ISLANDS

VANUATU

FIJI
ISLANDS

New
Caledonia
(France)

AUSTRALIA

PACIFIC
OCEAN

NEW
ZEALAND

North

West — East

South

Antarctica

ATLANTIC
OCEAN

INDIAN
OCEAN

QUEEN MAUD LAND

ANTARCTIC
PENINSULA

RONNE
ICE SHELF

TRANSANTARCTIC MOUNTAINS

ANTARCTICA

+ South Pole

SHACKLETON
ICE SHELF

ROSS
ICE
SHELF

WILKES
LAND

PACIFIC
OCEAN

INDIAN
OCEAN

Map Key
▢ Ice shelf
+ South Pole

Penguins in
Antarctica

Extreme Places

Highest Point
Mount Everest, Nepal (Asia)
29,035 ft (8,850 m)

Deepest Point
Mariana Trench, Pacific Ocean
35,827 ft (10,920 m)

Largest Ocean
Pacific Ocean
64,190,671 sq mi
(166,241,000 sq km)

Largest Lake
Caspian Sea, Europe-Asia
143,254 sq mi (371,000 sq km)

Longest River
Nile River, Africa
4,241 mi (6,825 km)

Highest Waterfall
Angel Falls, Venezuela
(South America)
3,212 ft (979 m)

Largest Continent
Asia
17,213,300 sq mi
(44,579,000 sq km)

Largest Island
Greenland, North America
840,065 sq mi (2,175,600 sq km)

Longest Reef
Great Barrier Reef, Australia
1,250 mi (2,012 km)

Largest Desert
Sahara, Africa
3,475,000 sq mi (9,000,000 sq km)

Hottest Place
Denakil Depression, Ethiopia (Africa)
Average temperature: 93° F (34°C)

Coldest Place
Plateau Station, Antarctica
Average temperature:
-134°F (-56.7°C)

Mount Everest